Chasing Wind

Chasing Wind

Finding Fidelity in Futility

Slade Nakoff

RESOURCE *Publications* • Eugene, Oregon

CHASING WIND
Finding Fidelity in Futility

Resource Publications
An Imprint of Wipf and Stock Publishers
199 W. 8th Ave., Suite 3
Eugene, OR 97401

www.wipfandstock.com

PAPERBACK ISBN: 978-1-6667-0823-3
HARDCOVER ISBN: 978-1-6667-0824-0
EBOOK ISBN: 978-1-6667-0825-7

AUGUST 16, 2021

CONTENTS

MORNING | 1

A NOTE | 2

SPRING FLOWERS | 3

SPRING | 4

FIREFLY | 5

BREEZE | 6

THE SEAMSTER | 7

RETURNED | 8

FALL | 9

PERSEPHONE | 10

SNOW | 11

HEARTH'S HEAT | 12

OF MICE AND MAN | 13

NO KING | 14

THE ROCK | 15

SEA | 16

LIFE'S QUEST | 17

FLIGHT OF THOUGHTS | 18

DISTINCTION | 20

REST | 21

HOPE | 22

ON TECHNOLOGY | 23

THE SILENCE OF FROGS | 27

ON LIFE | 28

WITNESS | 30

Morning

Air

Brisk, bites the lung

And welcomed in the day

Stirs something in the mind

Other than dismay

A

Memory of —life— once known

So vivid in recollection

How strange, what first met by sorrow

Supplants a bright reflection

Of

Joyful remembrance

As departed would have it

The path of grief, once well-know

Left for another, air acquits

A Note

Something can be seen—heard—
In the secret hours of the morning
If only sought, moves restlessly on, but
Time must be taken, of thoughts unhindered
To see the lark, The dew of the web
And understand one's place
In such things created, Not
Of mortal hands or mortal flesh
Nor, the fleeting dust that binds the mind
And this heart of stone unbroken, but
Of something greater than earthly desire
Something higher than can be
Fully understood, grasped, woven into words
For it is unwritten, and we are but
A singular note among the symphony.

Spring Flowers

Spring flowers fade to morning frost
Why do we mourn the bitter loss?
How does time make endings feel sweet?
For still, two coins is yet the fee.

Though our ransom paid by another
Fright remains quite an ever bother
Why early departure's so weary for those
Whose clock's fateful sonnet willfully impose?

Tick Tock –six o' clock and winding down
Till burdened weights hit the potter's ground
But even if delayed a day
Time always seems to get its way.

Spring

As flowers open up their head
I think upon what once was dead
Faded since, but yet in bloom
The sun awakens flights anew
Take off the sloth of winter's slumber
Exuberantly rising in brilliant number
The lifeless seed of last year's decay
Brings forth sweet fruit in colorful array
Seasons of dying light must come
Before that spring to life can hum

FIREFLY

Life is like the Light
Of a firefly
In the fading summer sky
One moment there.
The next gone.

Catch it.

If you can

BREEZE

Time is like a winnowing breeze
Determining what was there in truth
From what be left behind as seed.
So it might sprout with vigor of youth
Beyond the grave, if watered in its season
On earth, by the choices one makes
To love or to hate, whatever the reason
Chiseled in stone which never breaks?
Remaining inside our stubborn self-trust
We alone, with those first planted seeds
Discarded and left unmatured—to dust,
Return wages won from our deeds.

The Seamster

An

acorn sewn,

Reared, as light diffused through green leaves,

Its embrace felt —if ever so thoughtfully placed.

Will burst forth in new growth.   Seek the light.

And if allowed —after storms weathered,

Will try with wisdom granted,

To become the seamster.

RETURNED

Brick laid upon brick
Roads leading ever onward, cracking the earth.
But nature is never abolished.
Though hidden, often
Disregarded. Maybe lost
—For a time
Things once here, are not
And that which thought immoveable
Reclaimed by what came before.
A circle unbroken.

Ant and Oak
Spring forth in newness of life
A vigor unequaled.
The past returns.

Fall

Light heavy laden with joy,

Meets me in flight. A warming embrace

Everlong, shadows cast.   — stealing from what lie close
behind.

Abel cut down, colors fading.

Winter is coming soon.

PERSEPHONE

Death takes its mournful bite
The cold hand ever non-contrite
A withered tale is softly sung
Long before the morning comes

With the breaking of the dawn
All seems faded dead and gone
Life which seemed so full and sound
Now beckons on a still white crown

What seems the end, sure and true
Now is seen, the light makes new
Out of darkness comes the day
New has risen out of the fray

Snow

Small tracks in a snowy wood
Winding down a path recalled.
Soon fading from life. Erased
By that ever-moving clock,
To which our fetters bind.
But tranquility remains
In memory of us, who
In the falling snow,
Stopped to listen.
To that which
Transcends
Now.

Hearth's Heat

Wind and sleet beat against the
cold hard stone, surrounding
numb-red hands. Breath no longer
biting from frost laden air.

Warmed by the hearth inside
brought to life, by the joyful flicker
of fires enchanting dance.

As embers turn to ash dispersing
up the well-worn chimney,
the cold comes out to greet them
snuffing out their song.

Joyful moments remain behind
beating away old memories
soaked in bitter rainy days
which pricked tin roofs, till
sleep overcomes the cold
By the hearth's heat.

Of Mice and Man

Mice brawling inside the walls with loud cries
Stealing precious hours from my weary eyes.
By small relentless might deceiving
Does that little mouse leave me grieving
Of wishful strength in wanton supply
An endless night with such a war cry

Oh! How does your little brown portrait
Birth such dread in this well-built fortress?
And loath to see your nimble scurry
Across the kitchen in a hurry

What one would do to sleep the night
And rest in peace without a fright
I would find in the bright morning come
Delight in the lighted songbirds hum

Which now I cast away in shadowed blinds
The bold light of day which shall soon arise
The mouse in his dusky Marathon
Bested old Persia with his tired yawn

No King

The world waits.
For a time when,
Grip falls from God or fate,
Into the hands of men.

Their misinterpretations breeding
Ignorance of heart
Deceptive desires, misleading.

End comes upon Saul
And now in death's describing,
Turns to Paul.
Cosmology gybing

That which always was, still is.
And that which is, will be.
Man is no king.

THE ROCK

Seafoam sprays against
The rock of shore, immoveable
Tumultuous tides

Carried back and forth along the day
Tears like fangs in flesh
Each drop made of us

Ideas and progress play their hand
Time always takes its part
And yet the shore still stands unyielding
Unbound from hour or man

The word spoken to begin
Chiseled in that craggy shore
Pursued to the bitter end
For today, forevermore

Though beaten against
By scourge and lips
Not one line fades
From the word made flesh

SEA

Life is a sea
And I not the captain.
Tired and weary, drifting—
But not without aim.
Even still, it goes ever on and on.
What can I do, what must I do?

Follow orders. Unreluctantly.
Like the boy yearning for adoption
And to have faith, to trust—
That the captain knows, unfailingly
Where sea meets shore,
And when at long last the end is nigh,
Home is finally found.

LIFE'S QUEST

Life on this blue ball

Where flowers fade and bloom in —the heart;

of what is real, that arduous journey.

A quest or test it may be, To peer inside

each man: a question

Which yearns

for an answering call.

> To accept the father's love.
> Trusting through scars, well earned
> In relentless pursuit. By trust
> Even when grievous end draws nigh
> Deaths great bell in mourning rung
> The final race towards home is won
> And loving arms surround: at last
> They always will

FLIGHT OF THOUGHTS

Thoughts fly like monarchs west
Simple aligned chaos
While death stands single file
Each gets their turn in time

But this is oft forgot
With the passing of the sun
By mundane lives of one
Till that dark brewed tragedy
Befalls those held close
Breaking our melodical chord
Of monotony—

Forgotten

Not by disdain
And with that
The wonder
Of life under the sun
Passed away
By moments of
Here and now.

The now and went
Of bygone moments
Subliminally spent

Grab attention by the heels
And hold it with purpose
While sand still passes
From top to bottom

DISTINCTION

The lonely distinction between
Being and not
Is formed by muddied choices
Inside my mind and outside
Under the sun's firing heat.
How I treat other creatures
of clay and
The potter himself.
On this spinning ball of dirt
between two hands securely
Bound in a glaze of time.

REST

When my soul is made tired by
life's many troubles, I
flee to a cabin in the wood
to find my companion solitude
who guides me down, step by step
an uncertain path of self-reflection.
Through the long loud silence
of bright cicadas in fading light
the stillness of snowfall
and its blanket of simplicity
quilted by winding rabbit trails
warms my mind with humble
rest.

Hope

Red robin perched on a little branch
Darts in eventide with the fading light.
A motion so seamlessly contrived
Derived for purpose, I know not.
Growing things play their four piece sonata
While we go about each day.
Our home is right.
Here?

On Technology

O NE IS IN NO SHORT of company when complaining about the up and coming generations and their shortcomings, which to slightly older eyes can be glaring. This criticism must be done in a sparing manner though, lest it loses its meaning through over use and over exaggeration. So, when I conclude that the coming generations are using new technology in a way that, though may not seem harmful now, will have drastic effects to the psyche in the coming years. I do not wish to be beating another derogatory concept about young people into your head. That is not what I mean to do. What I do mean to say is that the unfolding of not only mental, but physical, and I might add spiritual consequences of new technology may even lead to a greater degradation of culture than the impact that the invention of AC had on Southern American culture.

When that conclusion is reached, one cannot without unquestioned bias, say that the problem did not start with causes that are in his or her generation, or maybe yet, the dominos started to tip hundreds of years prior, and it is not until now that the full effect of the small actions of great great grandparents are felt in full force.

The definition of technology that is in reference here is any physical object that is created to make a task simpler or require less "work" or effort to obtain the desired result. I do not refer to the maxim of progress as a whole but to the individual pieces that allow the puzzle of progress to be put together. This could be exemplified in the cotton gin by Eli Whitney, which, in and of itself, did not create the Industrial Revolution as a whole, but of which it was a substantial partaker in and created a great many effects during.

This can be conceptualized by a small boy throwing a stone into a pond. The stone is the new technology, and the boy is the producer. The boy knows that the stone will create ripples, but there is no way of knowing for sure how extensive the ripples will be. The producer, for the "betterment of society or quality of life" which is more likely, "the betterment of his wallet" puts out new technology without understanding how his product will ripple.

It is the use of technology without predecesoral knowledge that has caused ignorance to be bred into the users of technology. The blame of which cannot fall entirely on the producers, who are more worried about their own finances than the impact of their product on society fifty to a hundred years from now. Their disregard of the future for monetary gain is, of course, not good, but in a consumer-based society, it is up to the people to boycott products to which they are opposed. If the producers are not to be fully responsible, then that blame must fall upon the other interested party. The users.

Most of the time people go about their days using technology at practically every interaction they have with the outside world without contemplating its pervasiveness, history, or its impact on their lives. If you ask a person walking down the street today how a common doorknob works, I am sure you will get an answer, which will most likely start out with "of course, a doorknob works like" followed by a slight pause and maybe, if lucky, a muddled semi-correct answer. If you asked that same person how doorknobs have changed over the last century they would just be confused at your even asking a question like that and maybe say "why should I know the history of doorknobs?

What a silly person it is who contemplates such things!" If you went on to say that their lives would be profoundly different every time they reached for a handle if the invention of the doorknob had been in another place at another time by another person in another culture, they would be very confused. Even to take it a step further and say that the amount of time it takes for disease to spread in the last several centuries could be directly related to the number of doorknobs a society has, they would think you are quite mad. Of course, I do not mean to emphasize doorknobs here, but doorknobs are just an example of how the majority of us go about our lives, not thinking about the blessing technology can be, and also the inverse of how terrible the rippling effects can be.

By this, I do not mean to say that all technology is bad. On the contrary, I believe that technology is much of the time quite beneficial. It is my belief though, that technology is a balancing game of positive outcome versus negative outcome. In a world of endless advertising, positives are always thrown upon us. This is obviously the case in a capitalist economy when investments are involved. We should always expect the sugar coating or repressing of the negative . . . but we do not act like it. We go on not even contemplating the effects our smart phones have by being so close to our bodies all day long year after year. We do not think about where the oil that comes up from the roads right after it starts raining might end up. Western culture gets so caught up in "big" issues that simple introspective thinking is replaced by a smart screen, where we hang pictures of ourselves on mantles of pride that we call our "pages." Observation of what is around us every day, that sweet enjoyment of life which was once common place, is now subverted to a screen.

Yet again, I caveat that I am not trying to be wholly against technology, but I think that technology without predecesoral knowledge breeds ignorance.

—This is the common course of history.

When society was, for the most part, agriculturally based, new technology came in forms that were simple enough for most people to look at and grasp. As technology developed during the Industrial Revolution, there were machines coming about that not all people could understand entirely how they functioned. Still, though, they understood in a basic sense how the technology was made. As technology progressed further, dragging the people subconsciously with it, technology surpassed the understanding of the layperson and with it also went the concepts of its manufacturing. A gap has been created in the understanding of how technology works, how it is made, and common understanding. It has been taken for granted and not understood. Now, even the simplest of technology that was understood by all, is now lost to the modern mind.

An understanding of the past should go hand in hand with the use of new technology. A respect for the old way of doing things should be taught, so as to not be ignorant of the basics of life, while also incorporating the new which then creates a homogenous billet of broadened understanding. A type of understanding that looks at the stone before it is thrown and can see the ripples it will create and lives in accordance with that understanding.

THE SILENCE OF FROGS

Would the silence of the world be whole
If technology was a tadpole?
Or would that thin pane of crystal glass
Lay shattered on the quiet grass?

By our choices, and of others
We have cut our unborn brothers.
These willful wounds of ours will multiply
Ever increasing the bloody outcry
What once caught that crisp white vapor
Gave a name affixed to paper
Now all undone.

If only the clock could be unwound.
Before the fall to innocent ground.
What is done is done, and not by force
Since nature always seems to take its course

Yet, the mystery still lays
In cool, bright lit summer days
Ending under blankets of stars
While frogs sing long-winded memoirs
And stillness returns.

ON LIFE

WHAT IS LIFE? HOW DOES one describe it? By beauty or pain? An experience so common, but even so, is precious and of utmost importance. The stream of time that we are born in, going on. From whence it came, we are told. Where it goes we have but a glimpse. Every day seems taken for granted as if life were guaranteed. This is not so. It is almost as if we forget this. Caught up in the senses of the motions. The wise men of history teach us about the danger of this ensnaring trap. Can senses describe this life? Or numbers, letters, or abstract lines? Do eyes deceive or ears trick? If so, then all experience is called into question and subsequently nihilism is its end.

From my experience, it seems that the senses function on a swelling line. One develops senses as one grows in maturity. As time moves on, the senses eventually begin to gradually be lost, and one dies of old age. There is a standard. An order in the way human perception functions. It seems to me that if a man or woman has a differing way of perception using the senses, they are the outlier on the bell curve of human experience. This could be from a deformity or illness. They would be an outlier, not the median. I deduce from this that one can make an accurate assumption about the world around them in that it is ordered. Ruled. Written in a particular way, which does not deviate unless its deviation is a part of that overall rule.

If one goes searching for impartiality or objectivity, then do not run to a human. Bias is inevitable. Bias is the conclusion of pouring out experience into decisions of the now. It is an automatic response. It is assumption, but it is a logical assumption based on repetitive past experience. Without assumptions, one could not get very far in this life. Woe to the parents of an infant who will not make the assumption that the food in front of him or her is good to eat or the man who will not leave his home for fear of it growing legs and leaving him behind. We make assumptions about existence. These create memories and the ability to learn.

Life is like a piano recital where the notes are our impulses. We have free reign to play whatever we would like, however we would like, but Christ has come before us and laid down the perfect melody of what it means to live. Sometimes we play complex chords with multiple impulses, and sometimes we are given directions on how hard to play the keys. The amazing thing is that the Holy Spirit has put the moral law or melody on our hearts, and if we listen to it, our ears can discern when a note is dissonant or when it rings in harmony.

WITNESS

To them, a future witness be
where unknown grief passes growing eyes.
All that is now will fade away.

Fear waits at my door,
Calling to mind what could be.

I listen a moment, but joy awakens
Present hope in sprouting thoughts.
Of new beginnings.
A new creation.